Daniel Boone

SADDLEBACK
EDUCATIONAL PUBLISHING

Saddleback's Graphic Biographies

SADDLEBACK
EDUCATIONAL PUBLISHING
Three Watson
Irvine, CA 92618-2767
Website: www.sdlback.com

ISBN-13: 978-1-59905-219-9
ISBN-10: 1-59905-219-9
eBook: 978-1-60291-582-4

Printed in China

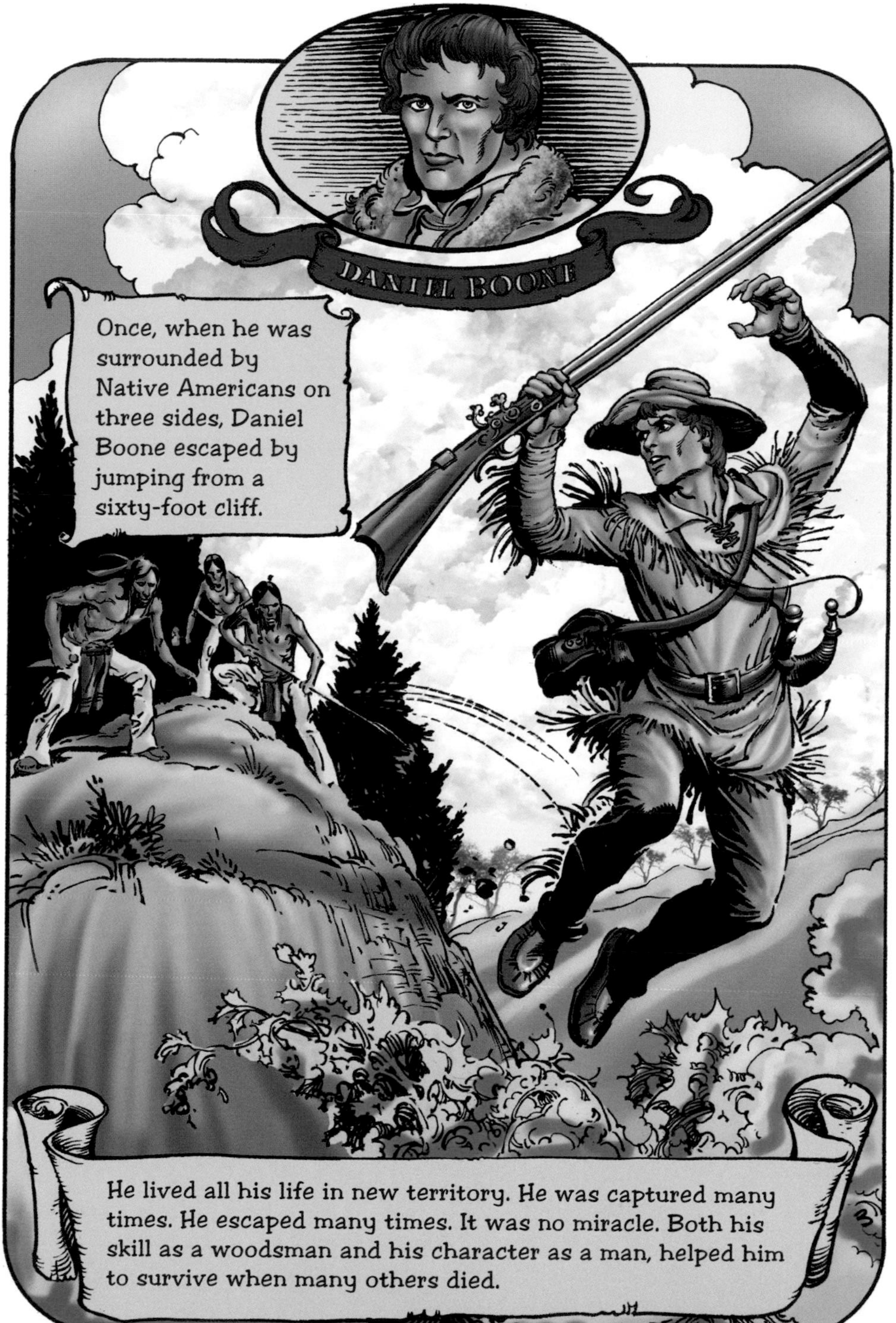
DANIEL BOONE
Once, when he was surrounded by Native Americans on three sides, Daniel Boone escaped by jumping from a sixty-foot cliff.
He lived all his life in new territory. He was captured many times. He escaped many times. It was no miracle. Both his skill as a woodsman and his character as a man, helped him to survive when many others died.

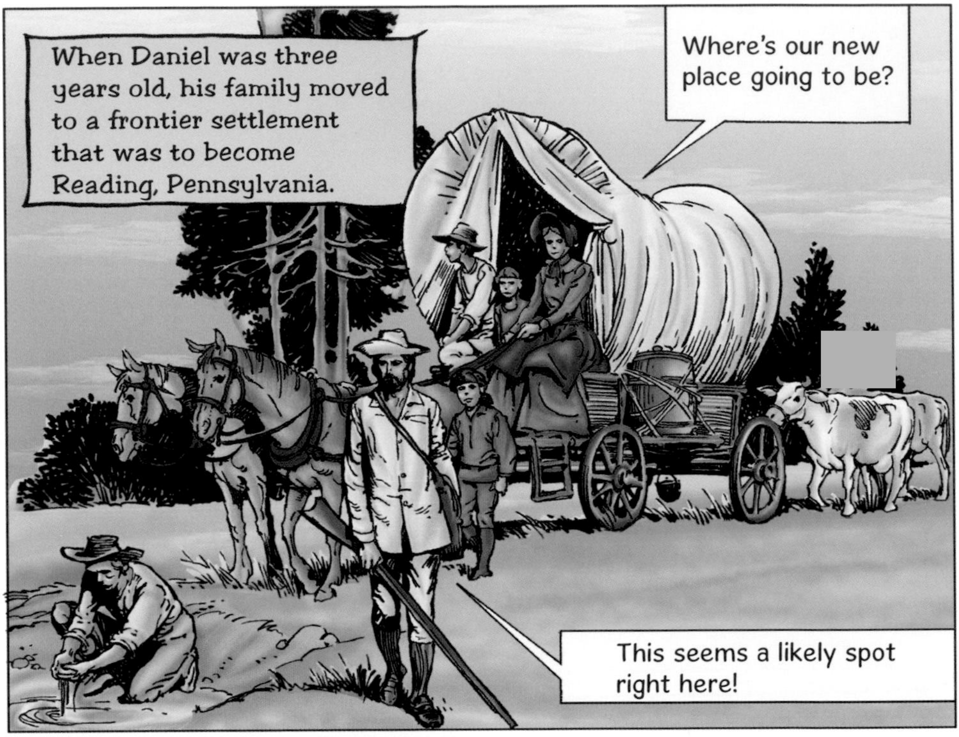
When Daniel was three years old, his family moved to a frontier settlement that was to become Reading, Pennsylvania.
Where's our new place going to be?
This seems a likely spot right here!

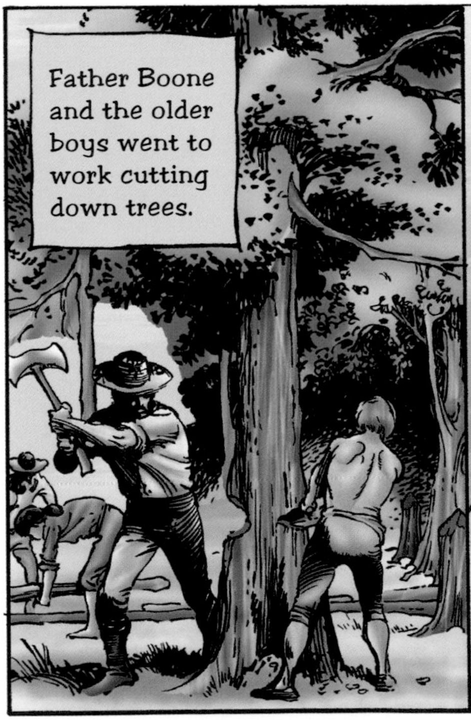
Father Boone and the older boys went to work cutting down trees.

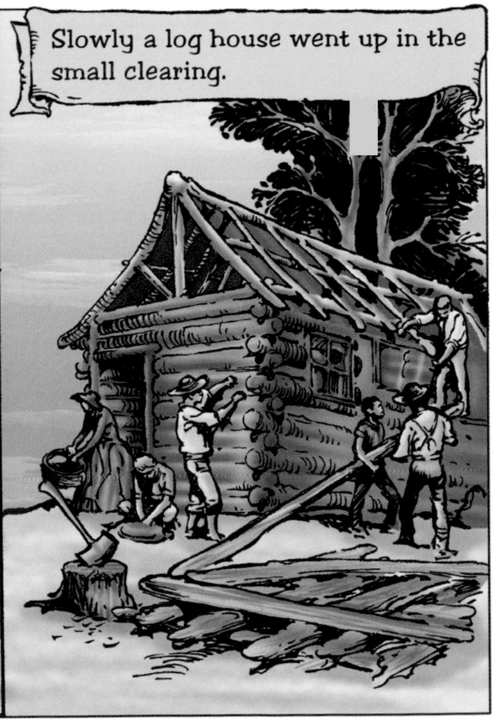
Slowly a log house went up in the small clearing.

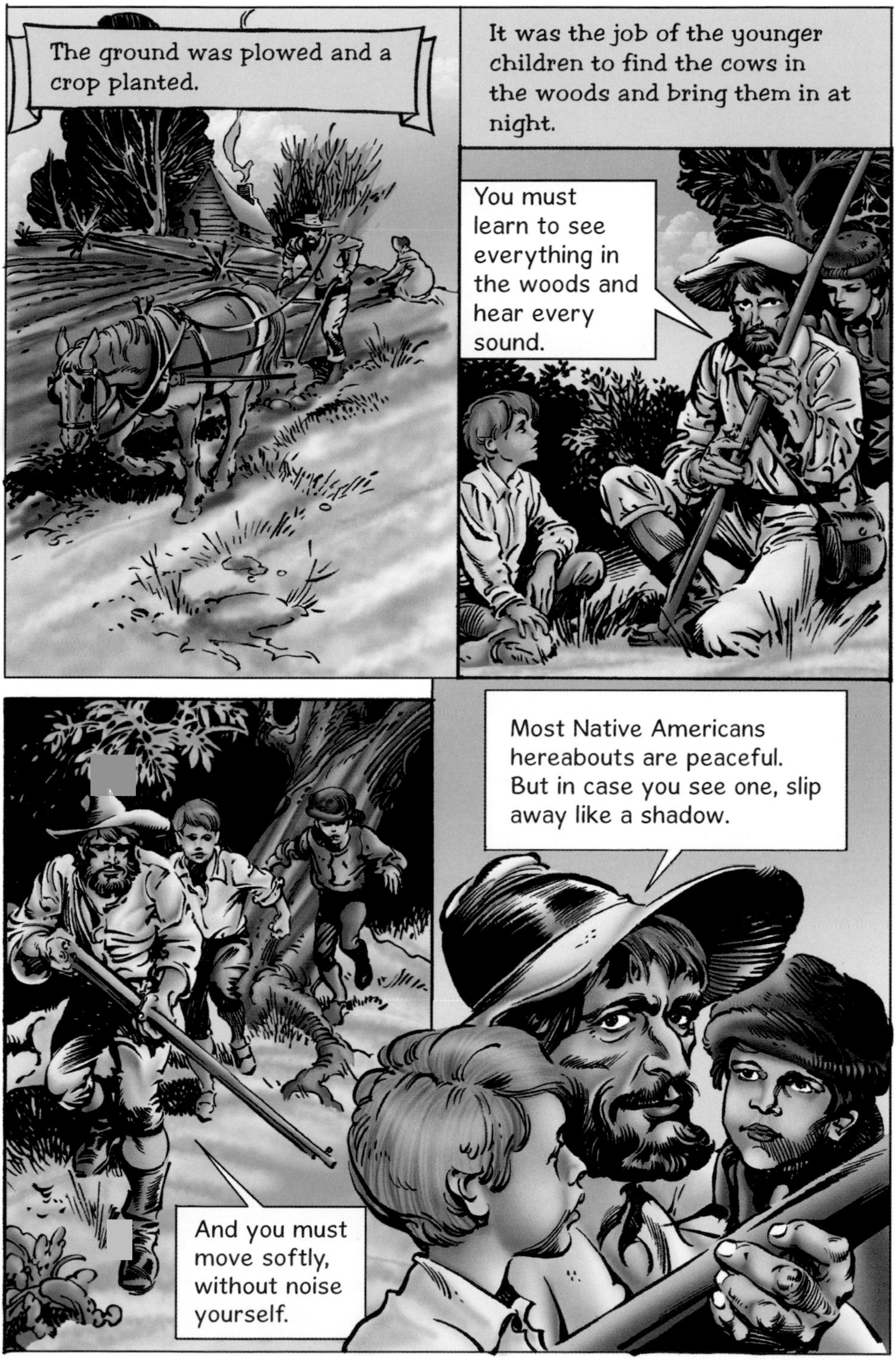
The ground was plowed and a crop planted.
It was the job of the younger children to find the cows in the woods and bring them in at night.
You must learn to see everything in the woods and hear every sound.
And you must move softly, without noise yourself.
Most Native Americans hereabouts are peaceful. But in case you see one, slip away like a shadow.

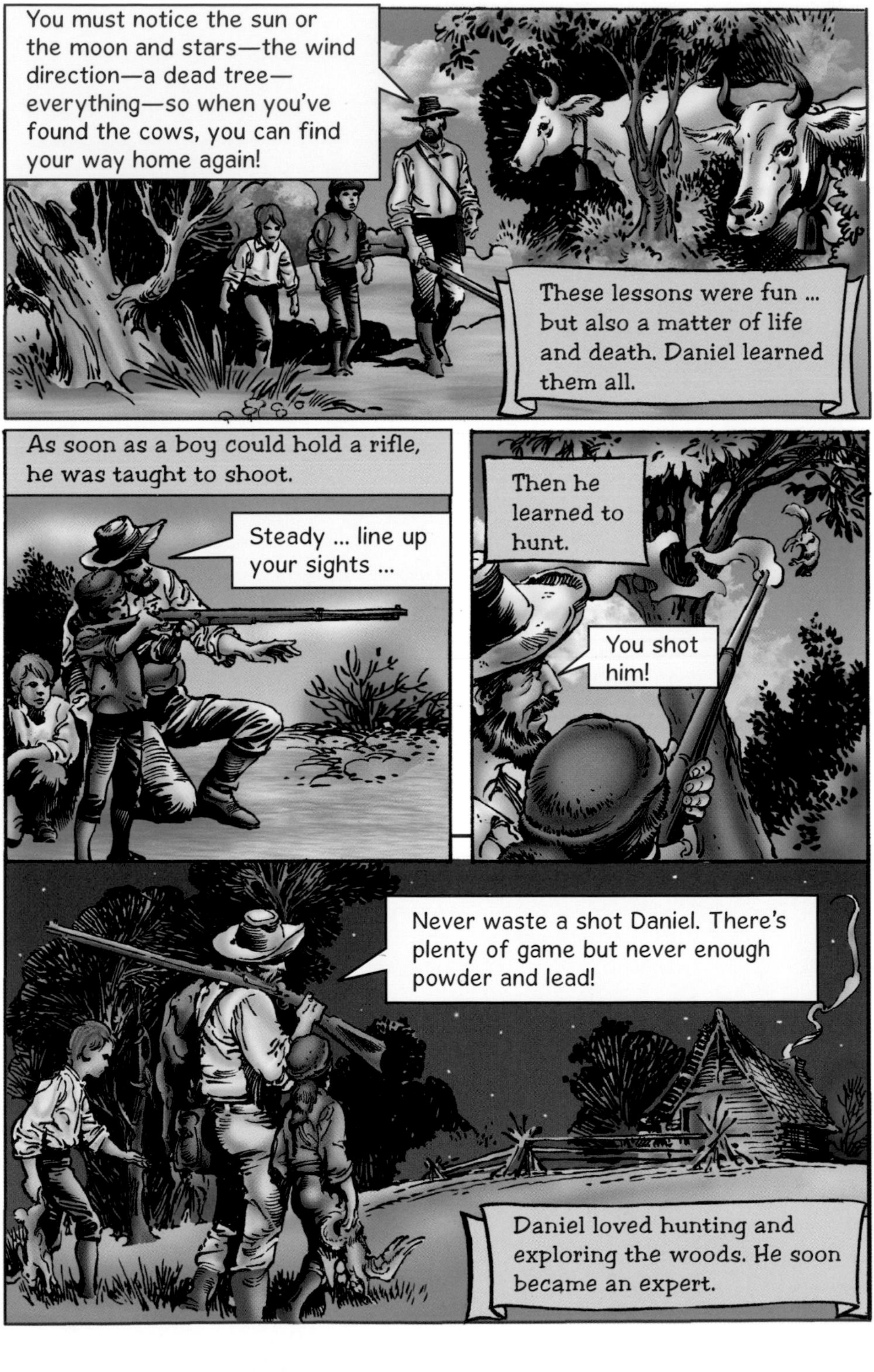
You must notice the sun or the moon and stars—the wind direction—a dead tree—everything—so when you've found the cows, you can find your way home again!
These lessons were fun ... but also a matter of life and death. Daniel learned them all.
As soon as a boy could hold a rifle, he was taught to shoot.
Steady ... line up your sights ...
Then he learned to hunt.
You shot him!
Never waste a shot Daniel. There's plenty of game but never enough powder and lead!
Daniel loved hunting and exploring the woods. He soon became an expert.

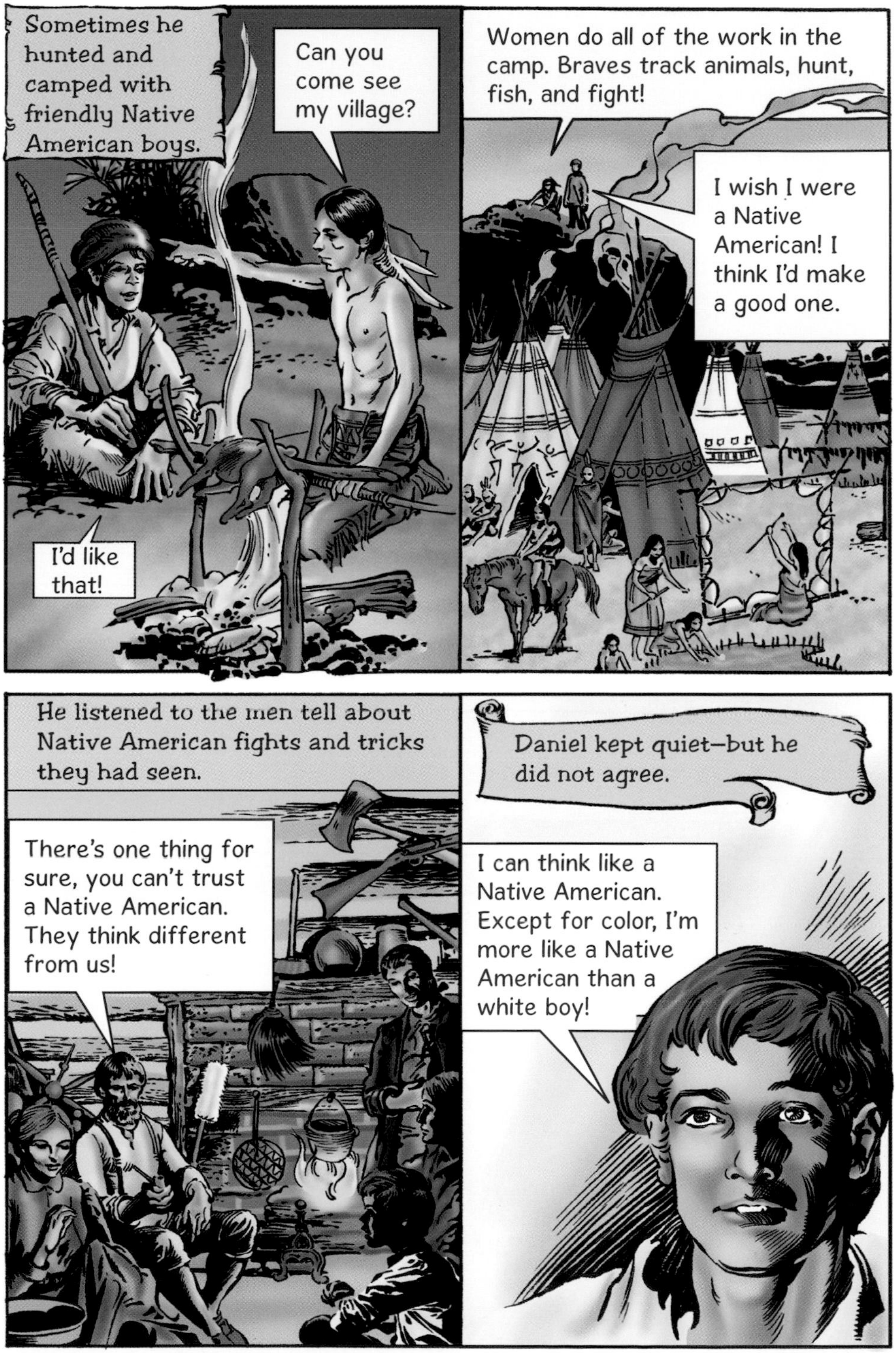
Sometimes he hunted and camped with friendly Native American boys.
Can you come see my village?
I'd like that!
Women do all of the work in the camp. Braves track animals, hunt, fish, and fight!
I wish I were a Native American! I think I'd make a good one.
He listened to the men tell about Native American fights and tricks they had seen.
There's one thing for sure, you can't trust a Native American. They think different from us!
Daniel kept quiet—but he did not agree.
I can think like a Native American. Except for color, I'm more like a Native American than a white boy!

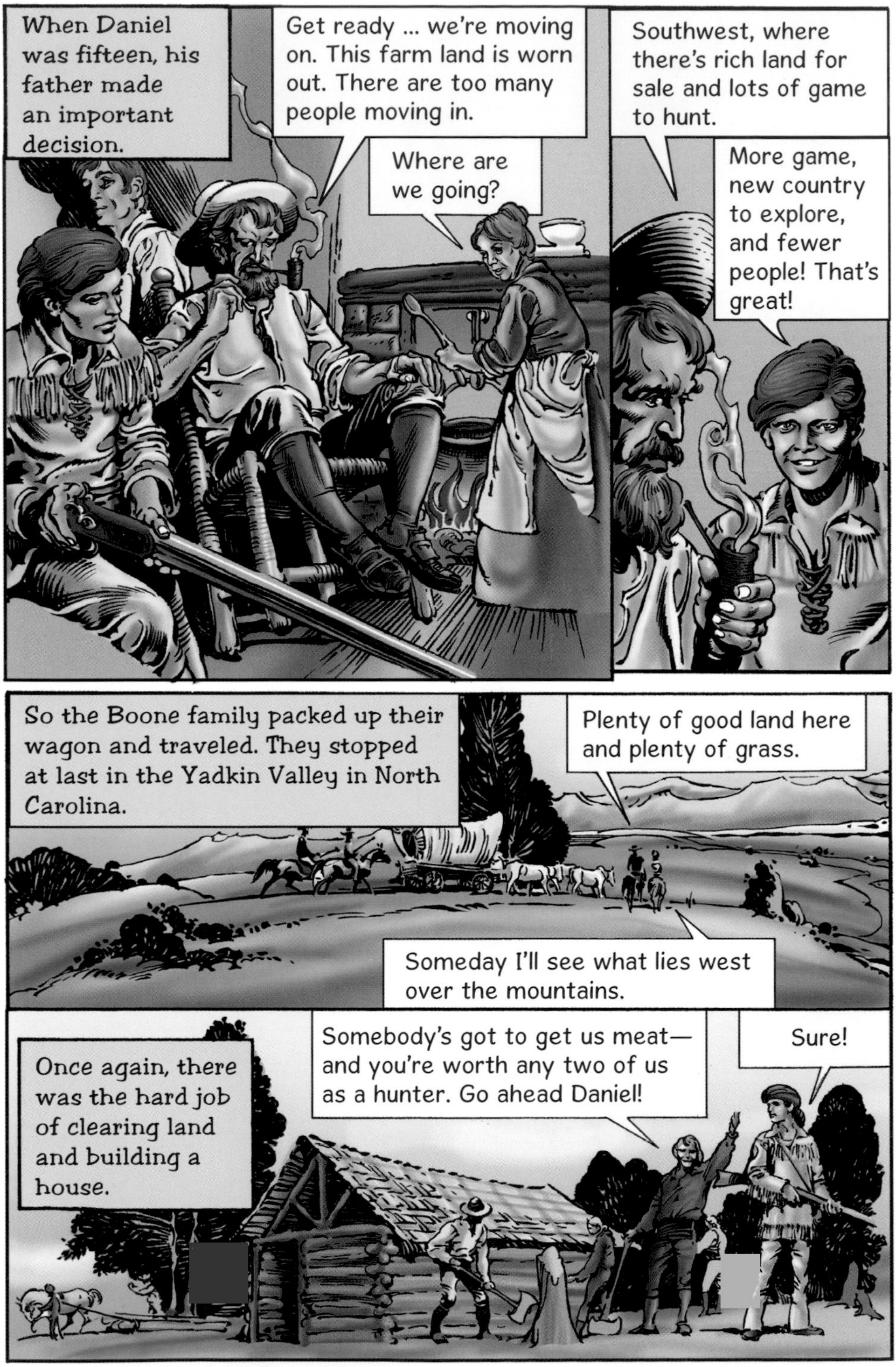
When Daniel was fifteen, his father made an important decision.
Get ready ... we're moving on. This farm land is worn out. There are too many people moving in.
Where are we going?
Southwest, where there's rich land for sale and lots of game to hunt.
More game, new country to explore, and fewer people! That's great!
So the Boone family packed up their wagon and traveled. They stopped at last in the Yadkin Valley in North Carolina.
Plenty of good land here and plenty of grass.
Someday I'll see what lies west over the mountains.
Once again, there was the hard job of clearing land and building a house.
Somebody's got to get us meat—and you're worth any two of us as a hunter. Go ahead Daniel!
Sure!

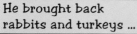

He brought back rabbits and turkeys ...

Often a deer ...

Sometimes a bear ...

The skin will make a fine warm cover!

Daniel grew up. Other families moved into the area. One was the Bryans.

Daniel, this is our new neighbor, Rebecca Bryan.

Soon there was a wedding.

Do you, Daniel, take this woman, Rebecca?

The neighbors came from many miles around to celebrate.

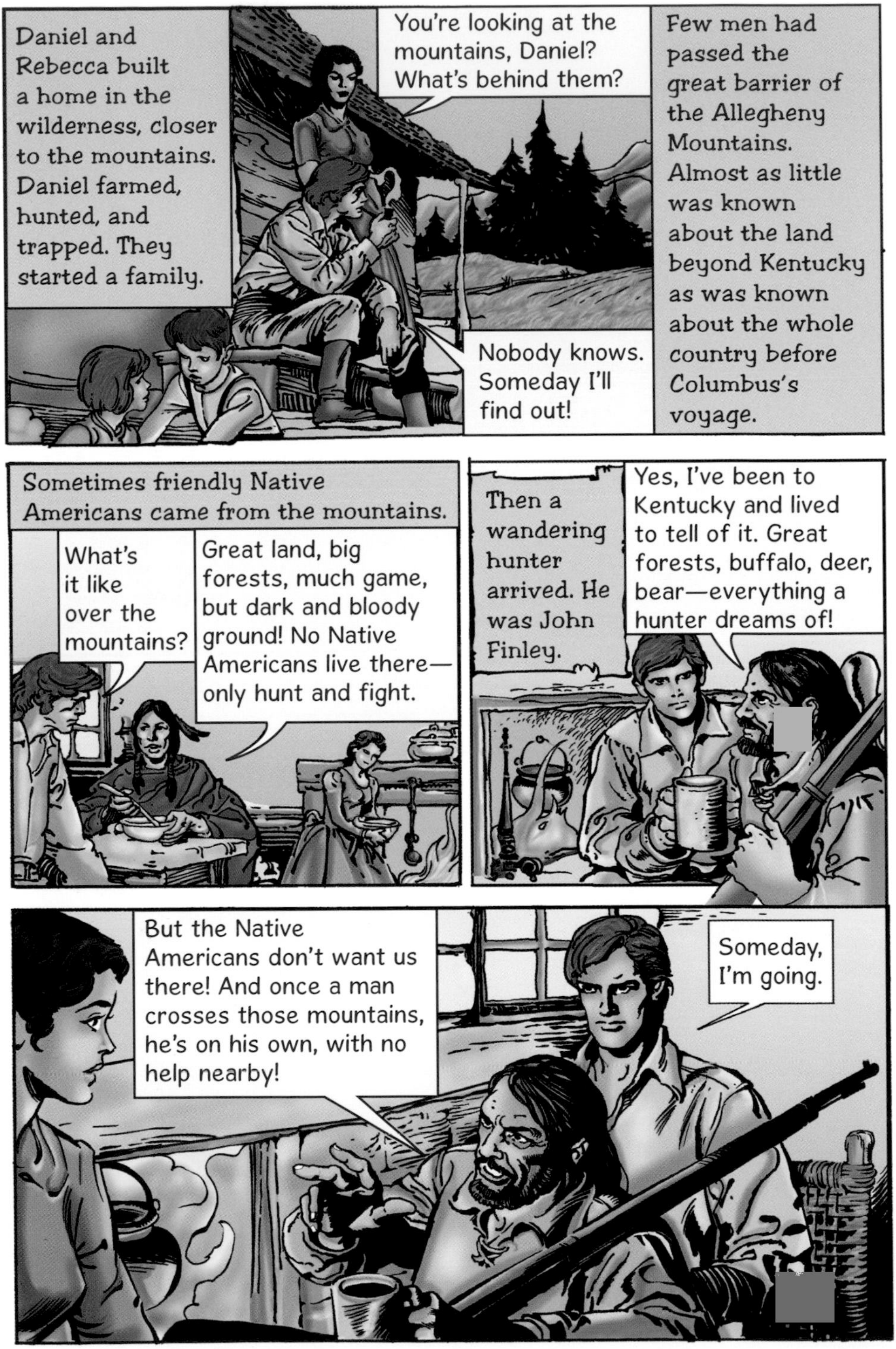
Daniel and Rebecca built a home in the wilderness, closer to the mountains. Daniel farmed, hunted, and trapped. They started a family.
You're looking at the mountains, Daniel? What's behind them?
Nobody knows. Someday I'll find out!
Few men had passed the great barrier of the Allegheny Mountains. Almost as little was known about the land beyond Kentucky as was known about the whole country before Columbus's voyage.
Sometimes friendly Native Americans came from the mountains.
What's it like over the mountains?
Great land, big forests, much game, but dark and bloody ground! No Native Americans live there—only hunt and fight.
Then a wandering hunter arrived. He was John Finley.
Yes, I've been to Kentucky and lived to tell of it. Great forests, buffalo, deer, bear—everything a hunter dreams of!
But the Native Americans don't want us there! And once a man crosses those mountains, he's on his own, with no help nearby!
Someday, I'm going.

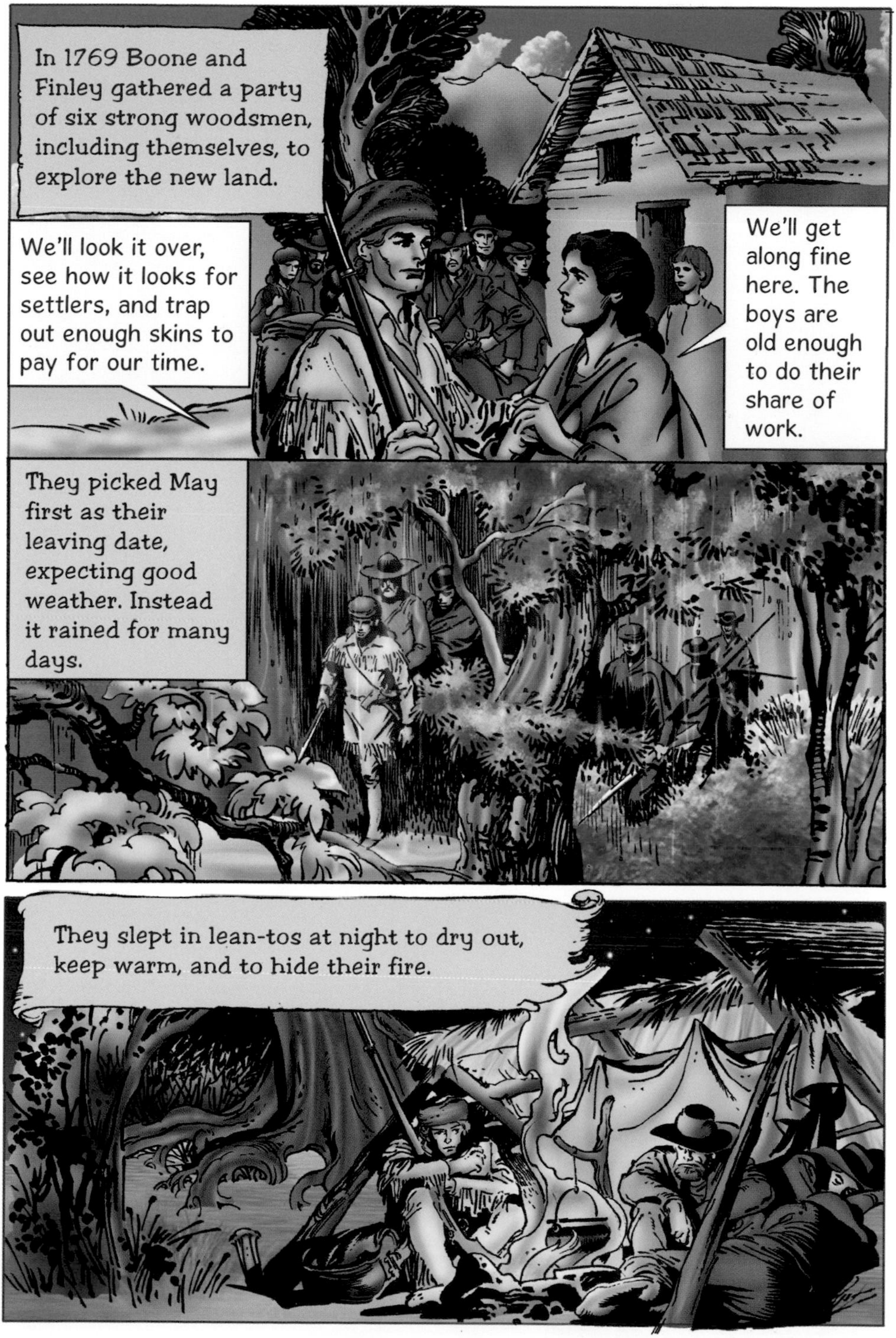
In 1769 Boone and Finley gathered a party of six strong woodsmen, including themselves, to explore the new land.
We'll look it over, see how it looks for settlers, and trap out enough skins to pay for our time.
We'll get along fine here. The boys are old enough to do their share of work.
They picked May first as their leaving date, expecting good weather. Instead it rained for many days.
They slept in lean-tos at night to dry out, keep warm, and to hide their fire.

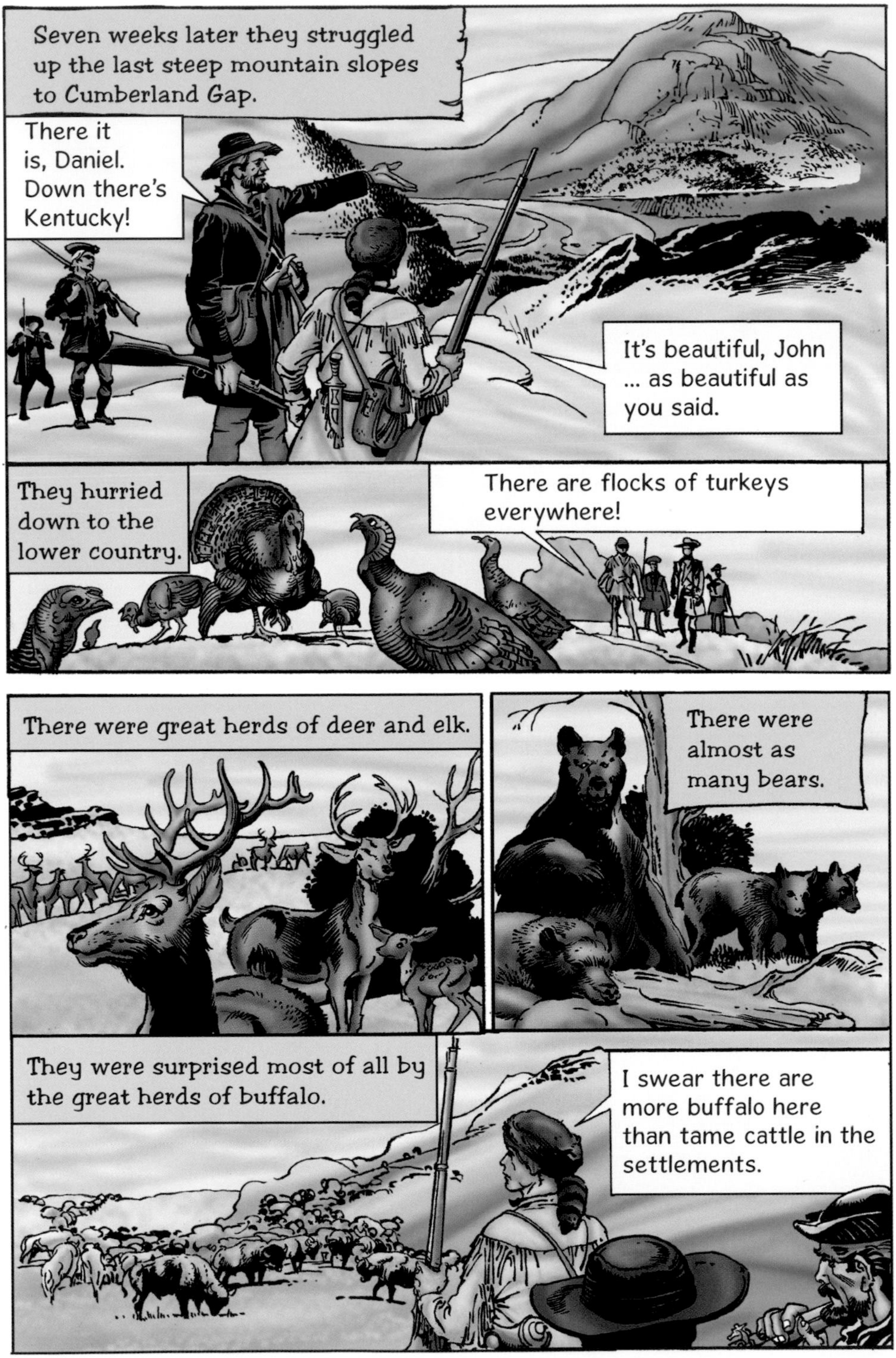
Seven weeks later they struggled up the last steep mountain slopes to Cumberland Gap.
There it is, Daniel. Down there's Kentucky!
It's beautiful, John ... as beautiful as you said.
They hurried down to the lower country.
There are flocks of turkeys everywhere!
There were great herds of deer and elk.
There were almost as many bears.
They were surprised most of all by the great herds of buffalo.
I swear there are more buffalo here than tame cattle in the settlements.

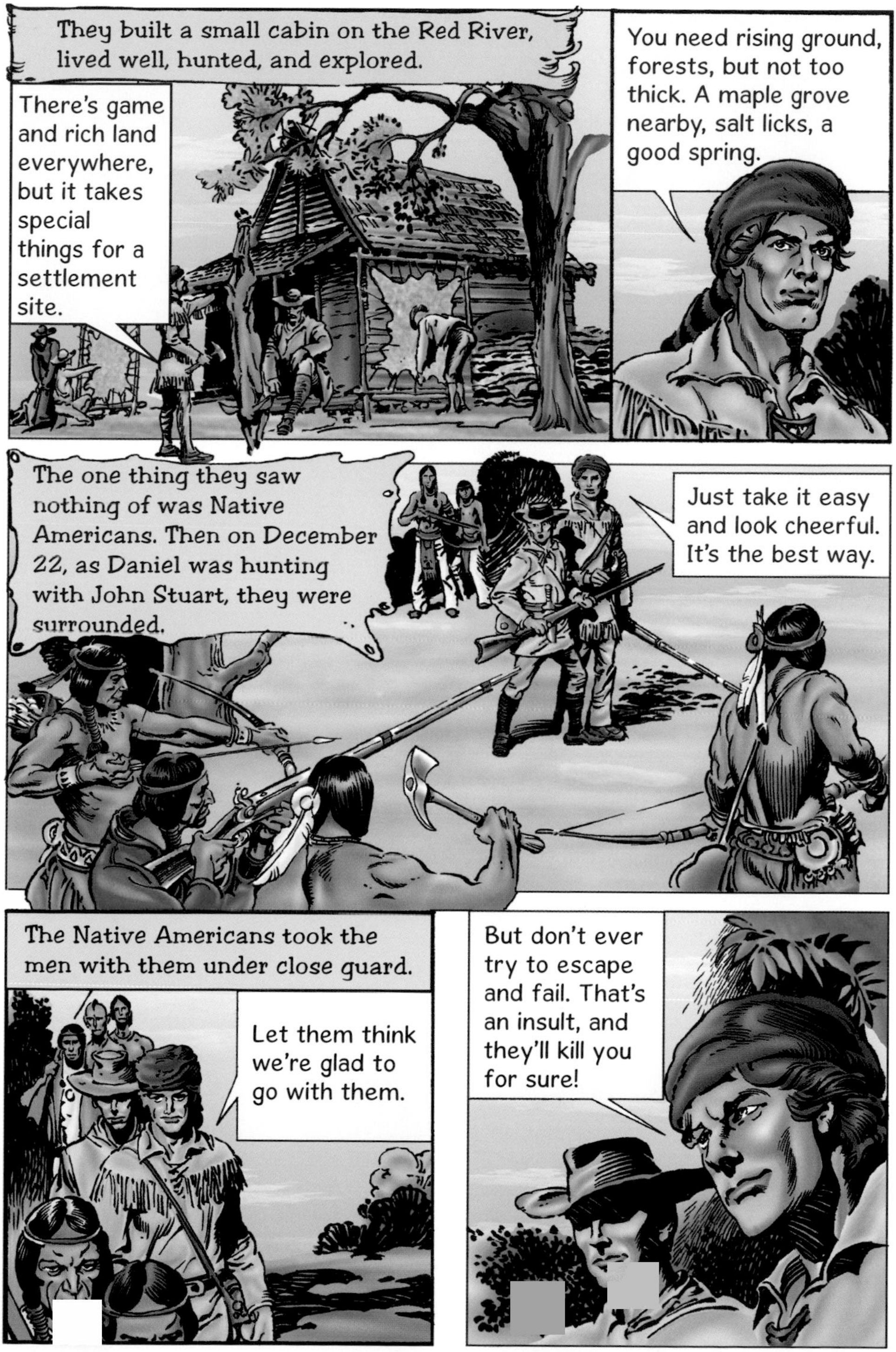
They built a small cabin on the Red River, lived well, hunted, and explored.
There's game and rich land everywhere, but it takes special things for a settlement site.
You need rising ground, forests, but not too thick. A maple grove nearby, salt licks, a good spring.
The one thing they saw nothing of was Native Americans. Then on December 22, as Daniel was hunting with John Stuart, they were surrounded.
Just take it easy and look cheerful. It's the best way.
The Native Americans took the men with them under close guard.
Let them think we're glad to go with them.
But don't ever try to escape and fail. That's an insult, and they'll kill you for sure!

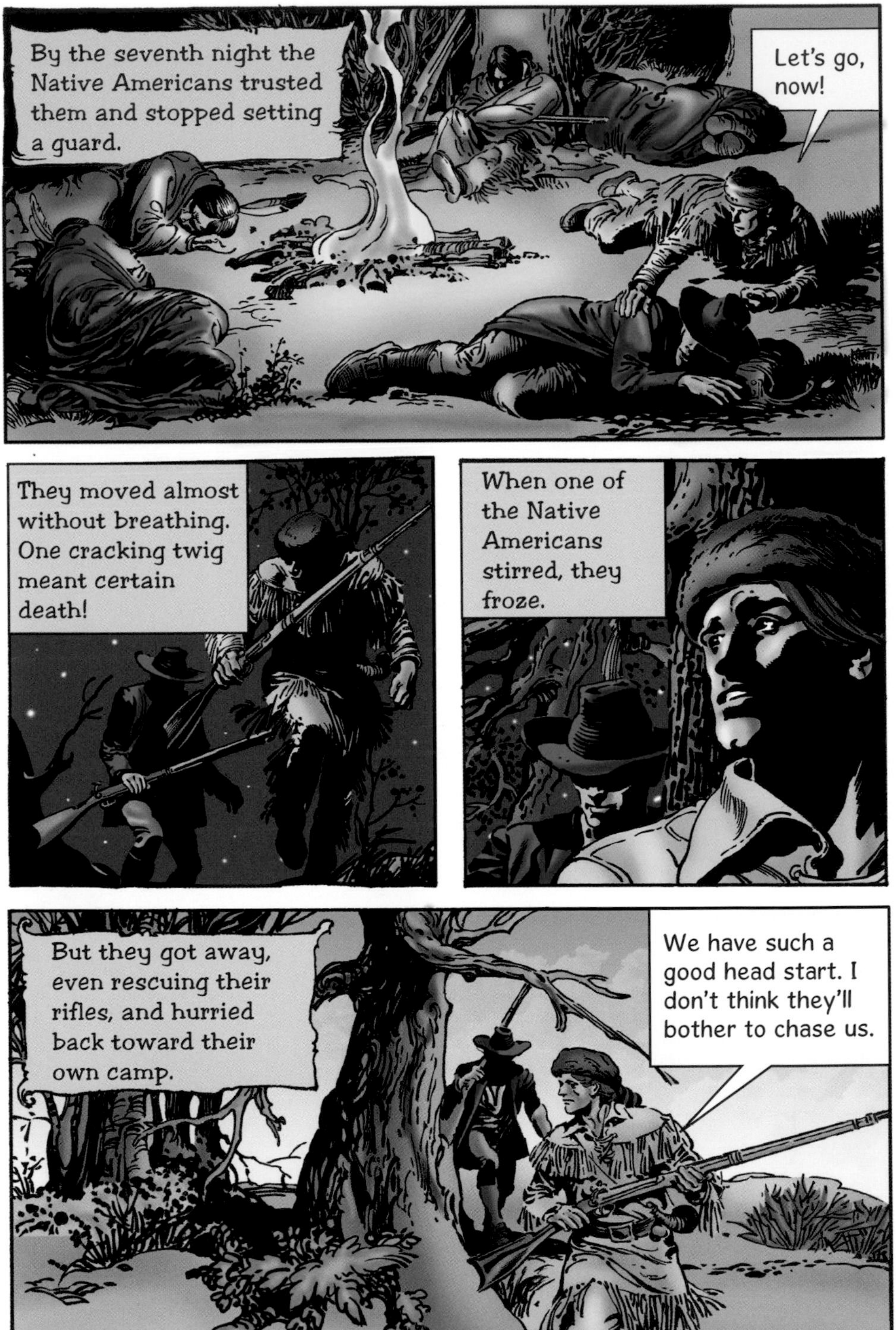
By the seventh night the Native Americans trusted them and stopped setting a guard.
Let's go, now!
They moved almost without breathing. One cracking twig meant certain death!
When one of the Native Americans stirred, they froze.
But they got away, even rescuing their rifles, and hurried back toward their own camp.
We have such a good head start. I don't think they'll bother to chase us.

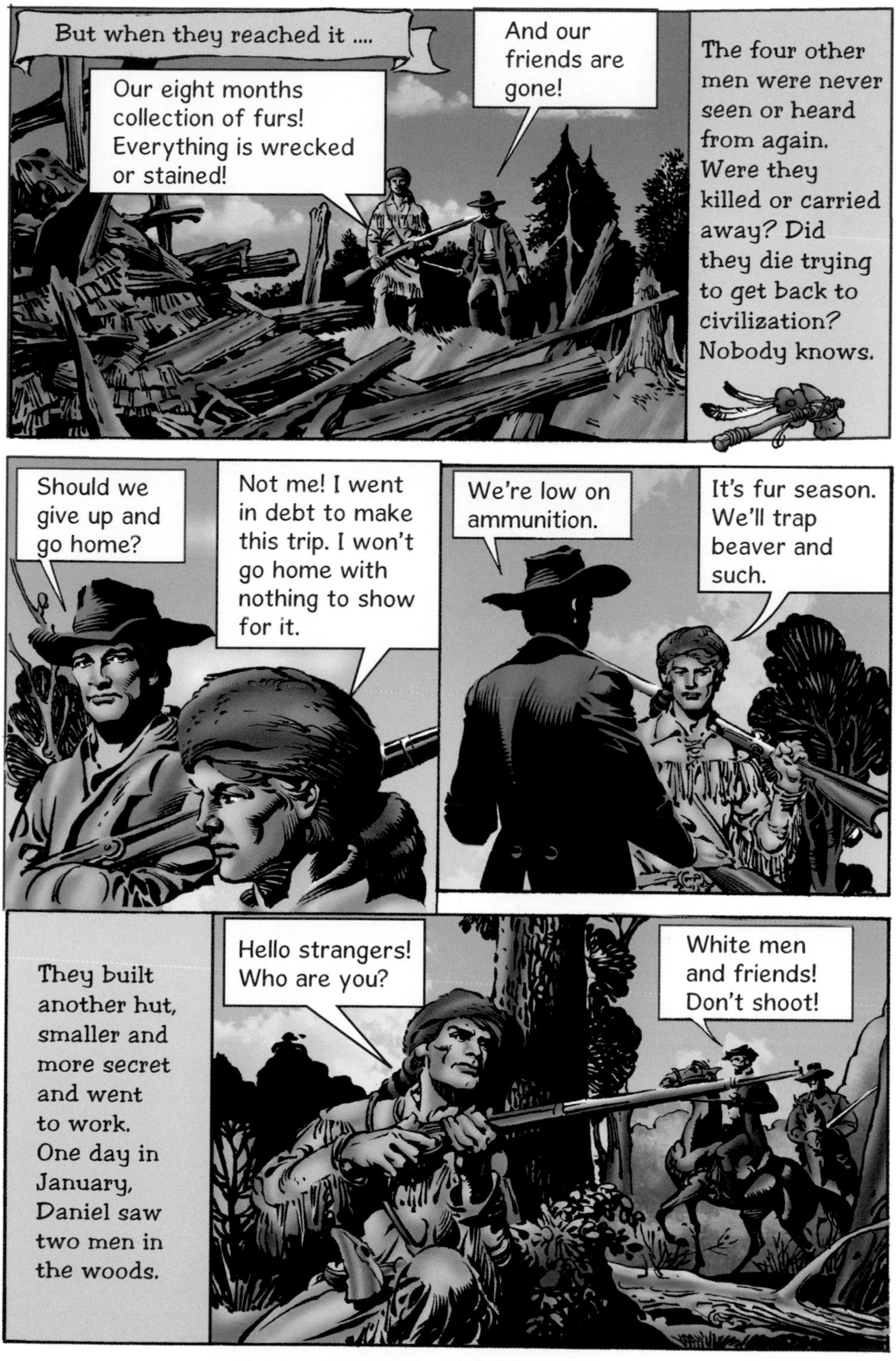
But when they reached it ....
Our eight months collection of furs! Everything is wrecked or stained!
And our friends are gone!
The four other men were never seen or heard from again. Were they killed or carried away? Did they die trying to get back to civilization? Nobody knows.
Should we give up and go home?
Not me! I went in debt to make this trip. I won't go home with nothing to show for it.
We're low on ammunition.
It's fur season. We'll trap beaver and such.
They built another hut, smaller and more secret and went to work. One day in January, Daniel saw two men in the woods.
Hello strangers! Who are you?
White men and friends! Don't shoot!

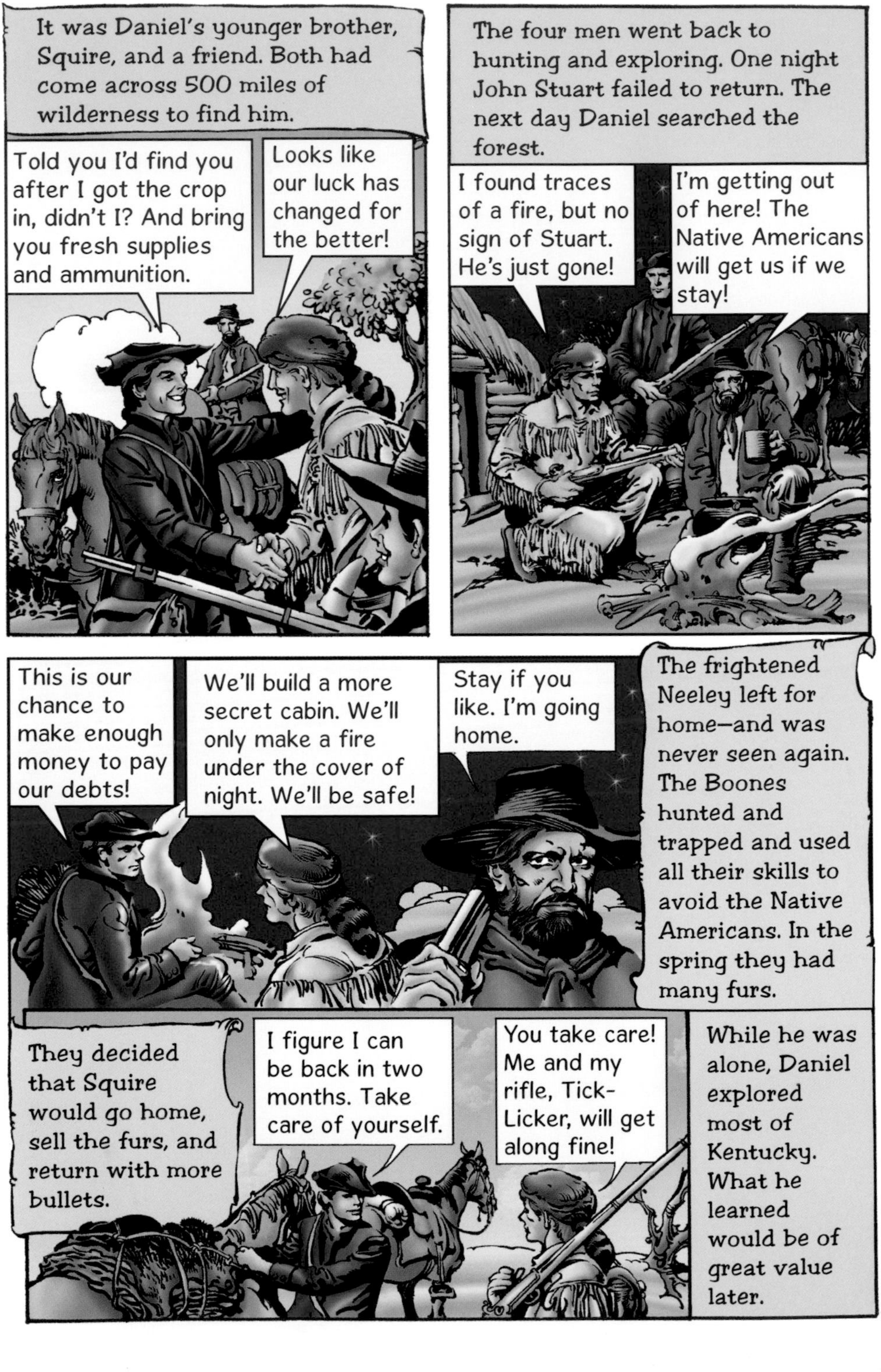
It was Daniel's younger brother, Squire, and a friend. Both had come across 500 miles of wilderness to find him.
Told you I'd find you after I got the crop in, didn't I? And bring you fresh supplies and ammunition.
Looks like our luck has changed for the better!
The four men went back to hunting and exploring. One night John Stuart failed to return. The next day Daniel searched the forest.
I found traces of a fire, but no sign of Stuart. He's just gone!
I'm getting out of here! The Native Americans will get us if we stay!
This is our chance to make enough money to pay our debts!
We'll build a more secret cabin. We'll only make a fire under the cover of night. We'll be safe!
Stay if you like. I'm going home.
The frightened Neeley left for home—and was never seen again. The Boones hunted and trapped and used all their skills to avoid the Native Americans. In the spring they had many furs.
They decided that Squire would go home, sell the furs, and return with more bullets.
I figure I can be back in two months. Take care of yourself.
You take care! Me and my rifle, Tick-Licker, will get along fine!
While he was alone, Daniel explored most of Kentucky. What he learned would be of great value later.

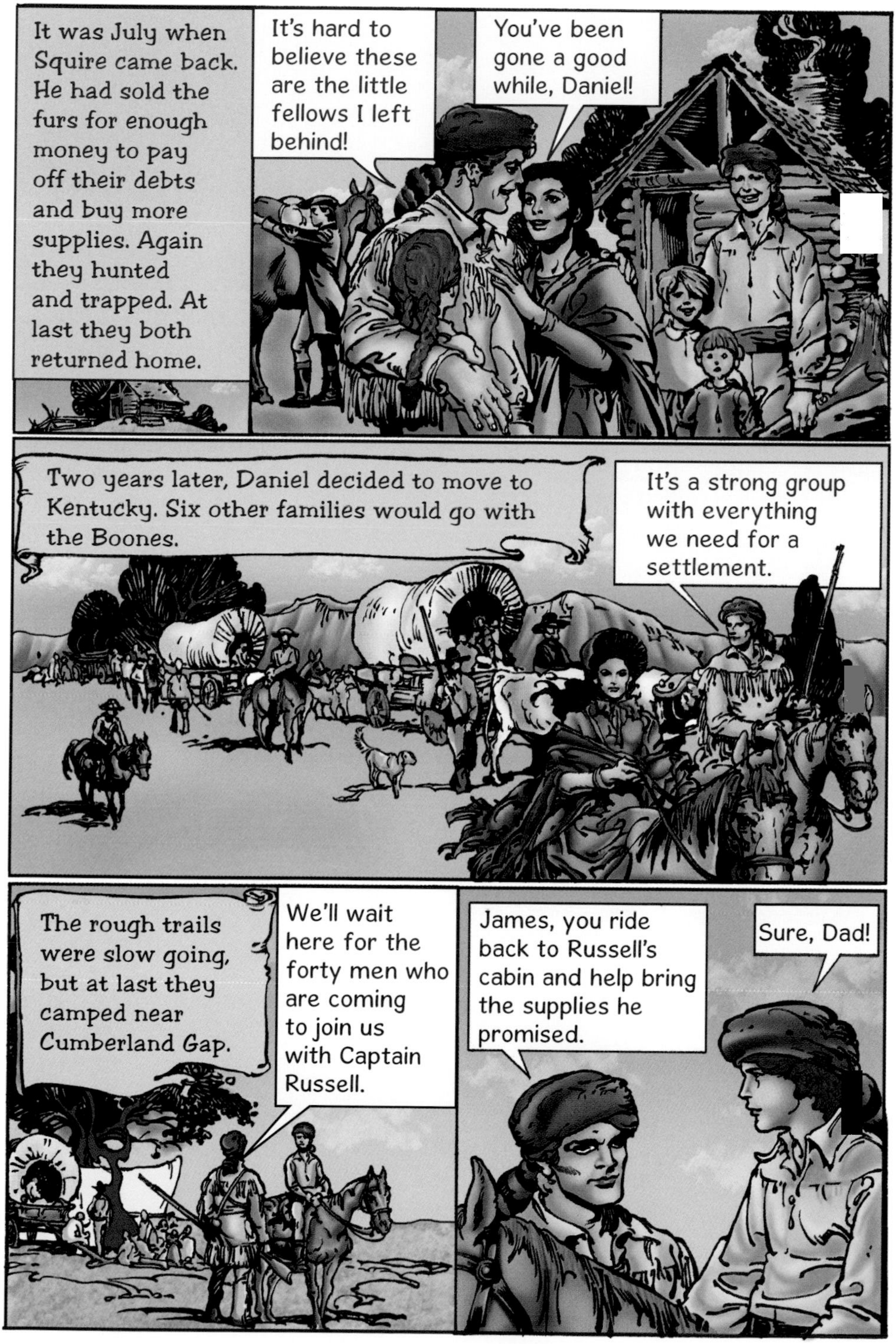
It was July when Squire came back. He had sold the furs for enough money to pay off their debts and buy more supplies. Again they hunted and trapped. At last they both returned home.
It's hard to believe these are the little fellows I left behind!
You've been gone a good while, Daniel!
Two years later, Daniel decided to move to Kentucky. Six other families would go with the Boones.
It's a strong group with everything we need for a settlement.
The rough trails were slow going, but at last they camped near Cumberland Gap.
We'll wait here for the forty men who are coming to join us with Captain Russell.
James, you ride back to Russell's cabin and help bring the supplies he promised.
Sure, Dad!

On the way back from Russell's, James Boone and the men with him camped overnight. A Shawnee war party surprised them at daybreak.

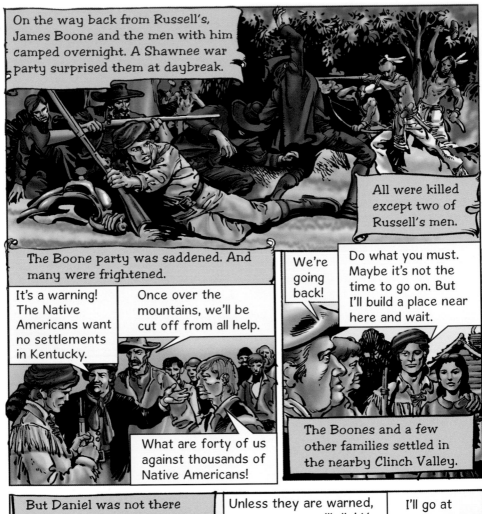

All were killed except two of Russell's men.

The Boone party was saddened. And many were frightened.

It's a warning! The Native Americans want no settlements in Kentucky.

Once over the mountains, we'll be cut off from all help.

What are forty of us against thousands of Native Americans!

We're going back!

Do what you must. Maybe it's not the time to go on. But I'll build a place near here and wait.

The Boones and a few other families settled in the nearby Clinch Valley.

But Daniel was not there long. He was sent for by Lord Dunmore, the Governor of Virginia.

I have sent parties into Kentucky to survey the land. Now the Native Americans there have started attacking all the white men they find.

Unless they are warned, my surveyors will die! You are the only man who might reach them and lead them to safety.

I'll go at once.

Covering 800 miles in two months on foot, Daniel reached the surveyors and led them out by secret ways.

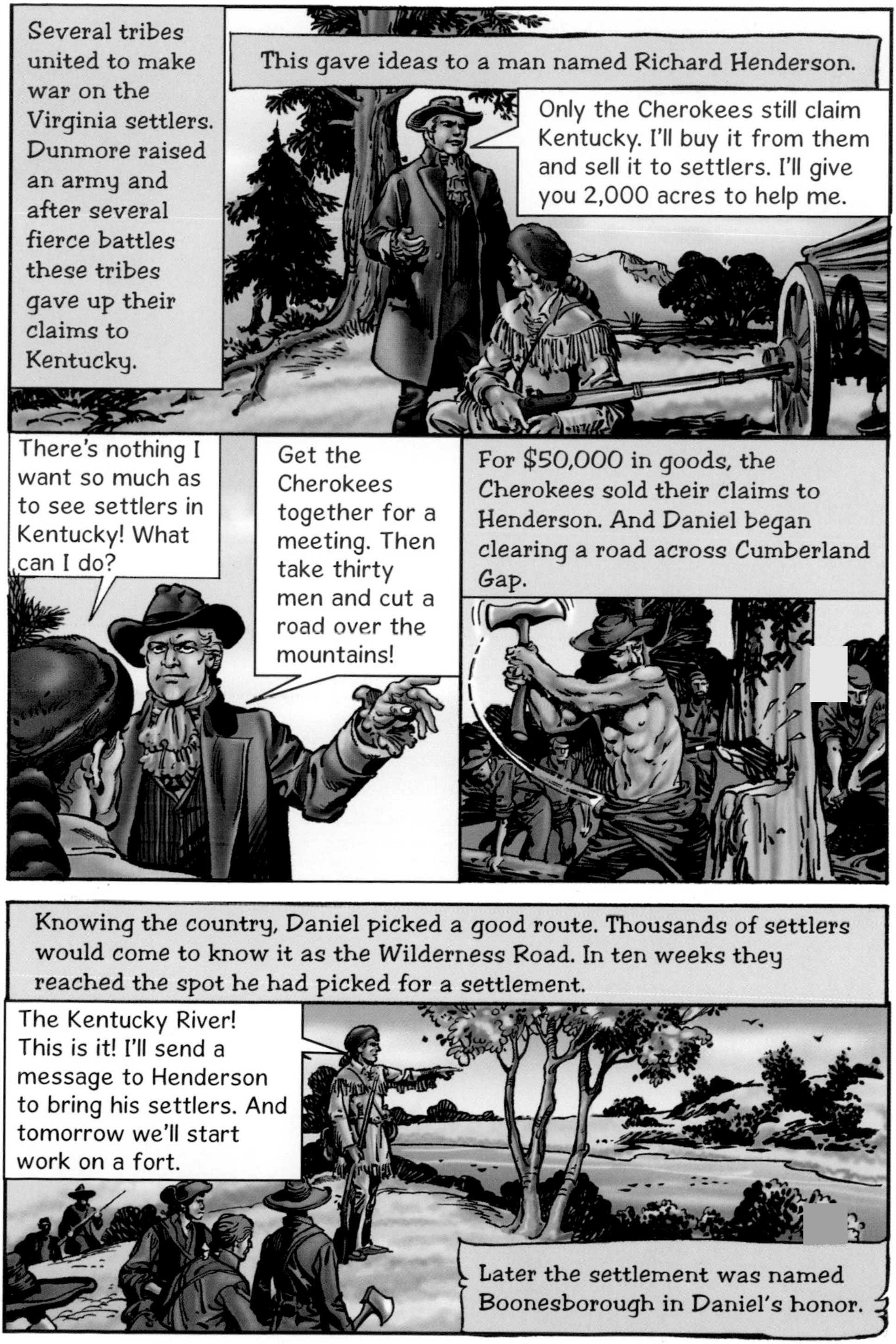
Several tribes united to make war on the Virginia settlers. Dunmore raised an army and after several fierce battles these tribes gave up their claims to Kentucky.
This gave ideas to a man named Richard Henderson.
Only the Cherokees still claim Kentucky. I'll buy it from them and sell it to settlers. I'll give you 2,000 acres to help me.
There's nothing I want so much as to see settlers in Kentucky! What can I do?
Get the Cherokees together for a meeting. Then take thirty men and cut a road over the mountains!
For $50,000 in goods, the Cherokees sold their claims to Henderson. And Daniel began clearing a road across Cumberland Gap.
Knowing the country, Daniel picked a good route. Thousands of settlers would come to know it as the Wilderness Road. In ten weeks they reached the spot he had picked for a settlement.
The Kentucky River! This is it! I'll send a message to Henderson to bring his settlers. And tomorrow we'll start work on a fort.
Later the settlement was named Boonesborough in Daniel's honor.

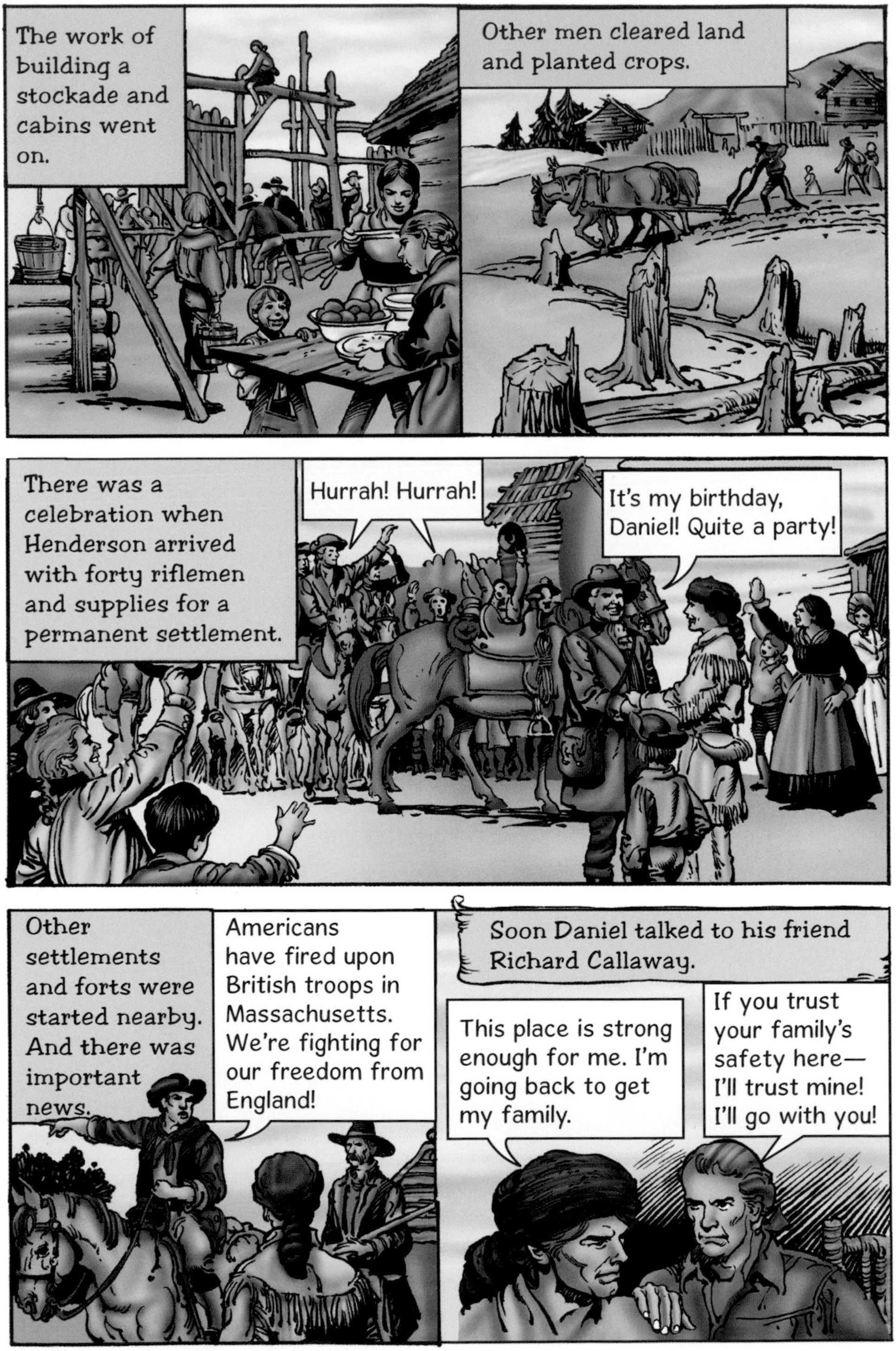

The work of building a stockade and cabins went on.
Other men cleared land and planted crops.
There was a celebration when Henderson arrived with forty riflemen and supplies for a permanent settlement.
Hurrah! Hurrah!
It's my birthday, Daniel! Quite a party!
Other settlements and forts were started nearby. And there was important news.
Americans have fired upon British troops in Massachusetts. We're fighting for our freedom from England!
Soon Daniel talked to his friend Richard Callaway.
This place is strong enough for me. I'm going back to get my family.
If you trust your family's safety here— I'll trust mine! I'll go with you!

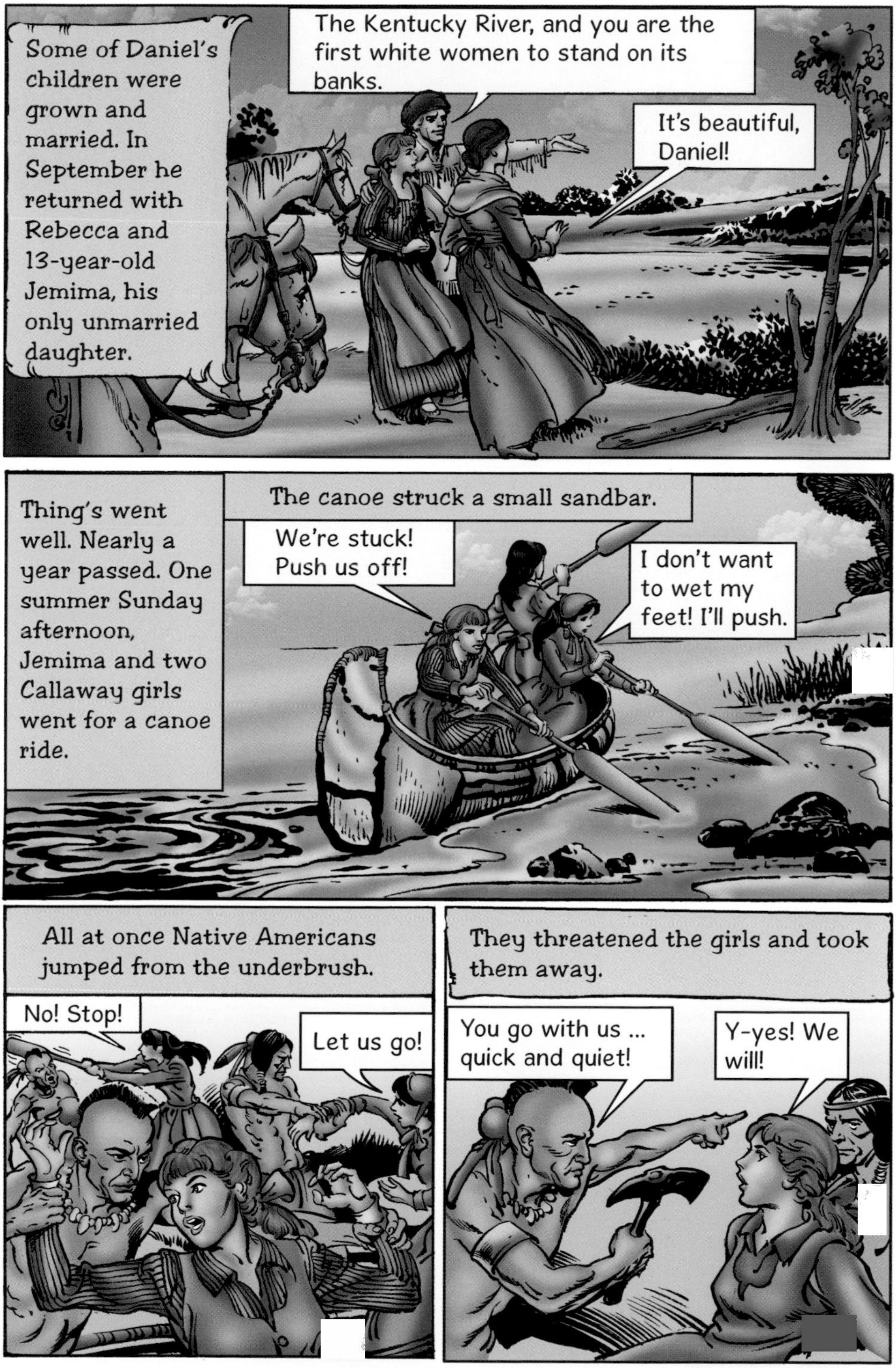
Some of Daniel's children were grown and married. In September he returned with Rebecca and 13-year-old Jemima, his only unmarried daughter.
The Kentucky River, and you are the first white women to stand on its banks.
It's beautiful, Daniel!
Thing's went well. Nearly a year passed. One summer Sunday afternoon, Jemima and two Callaway girls went for a canoe ride.
The canoe struck a small sandbar.
We're stuck! Push us off!
I don't want to wet my feet! I'll push.
All at once Native Americans jumped from the underbrush.
No! Stop!
Let us go!
They threatened the girls and took them away.
You go with us ... quick and quiet!
Y-yes! We will!

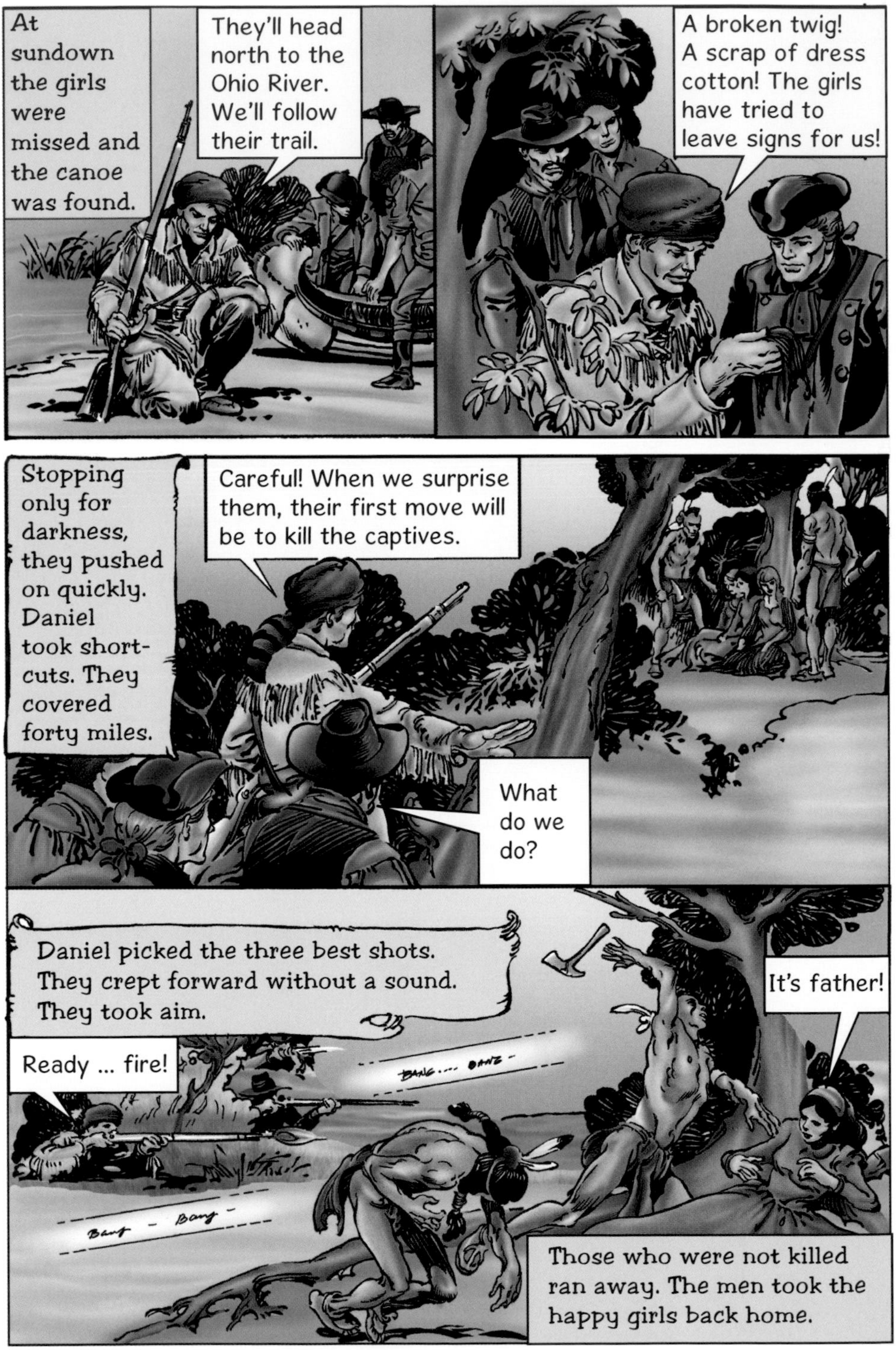
At sundown the girls were missed and the canoe was found.
They'll head north to the Ohio River. We'll follow their trail.
A broken twig! A scrap of dress cotton! The girls have tried to leave signs for us!
Stopping only for darkness, they pushed on quickly. Daniel took short-cuts. They covered forty miles.
Careful! When we surprise them, their first move will be to kill the captives.
What do we do?
Daniel picked the three best shots. They crept forward without a sound. They took aim.
Ready ... fire!
It's father!
Bang – Bang
Those who were not killed ran away. The men took the happy girls back home.

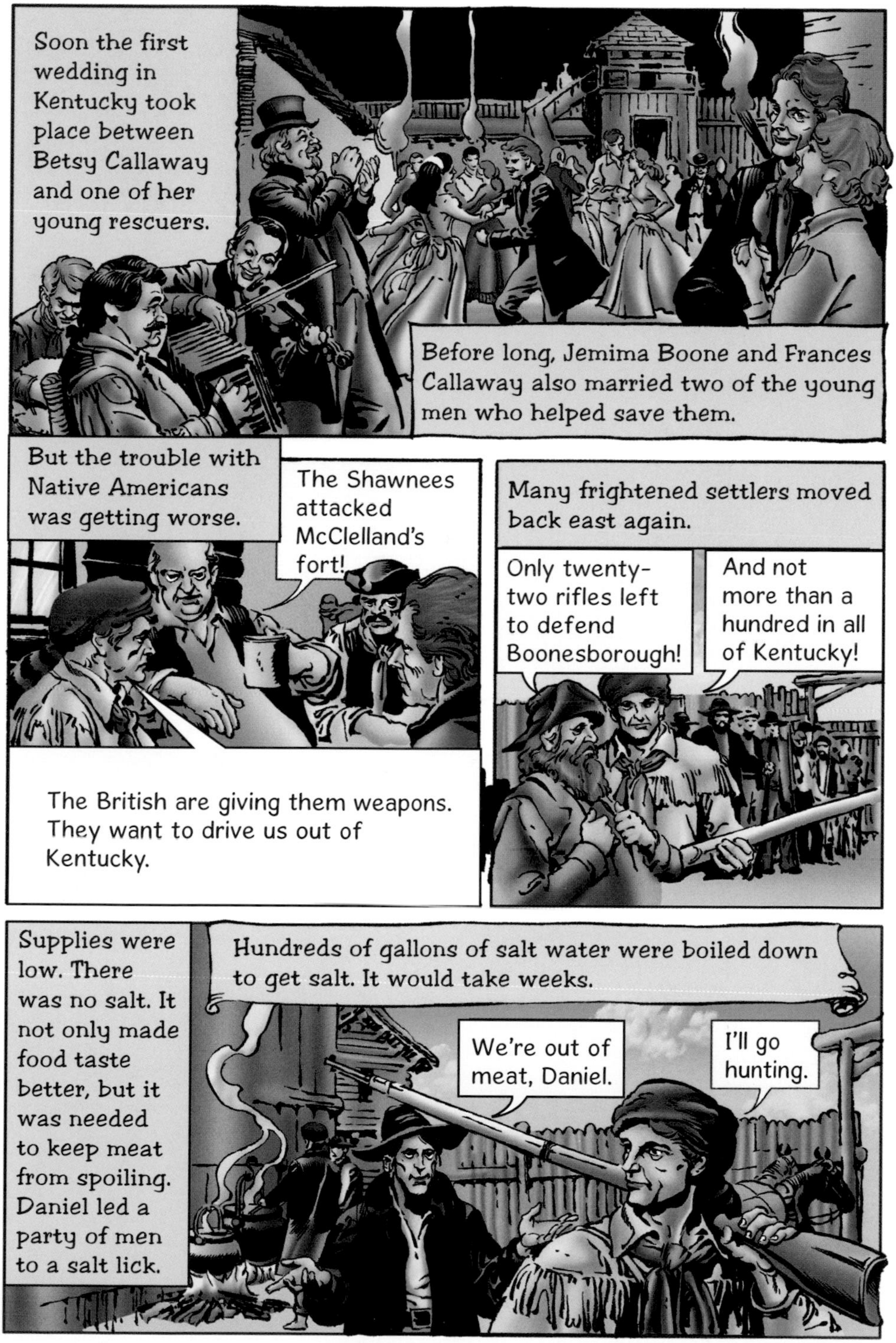
Soon the first wedding in Kentucky took place between Betsy Callaway and one of her young rescuers.
Before long, Jemima Boone and Frances Callaway also married two of the young men who helped save them.
But the trouble with Native Americans was getting worse.
The Shawnees attacked McClelland's fort!
The British are giving them weapons. They want to drive us out of Kentucky.
Many frightened settlers moved back east again.
Only twenty-two rifles left to defend Boonesborough!
And not more than a hundred in all of Kentucky!
Supplies were low. There was no salt. It not only made food taste better, but it was needed to keep meat from spoiling. Daniel led a party of men to a salt lick.
Hundreds of gallons of salt water were boiled down to get salt. It would take weeks.
We're out of meat, Daniel.
I'll go hunting.

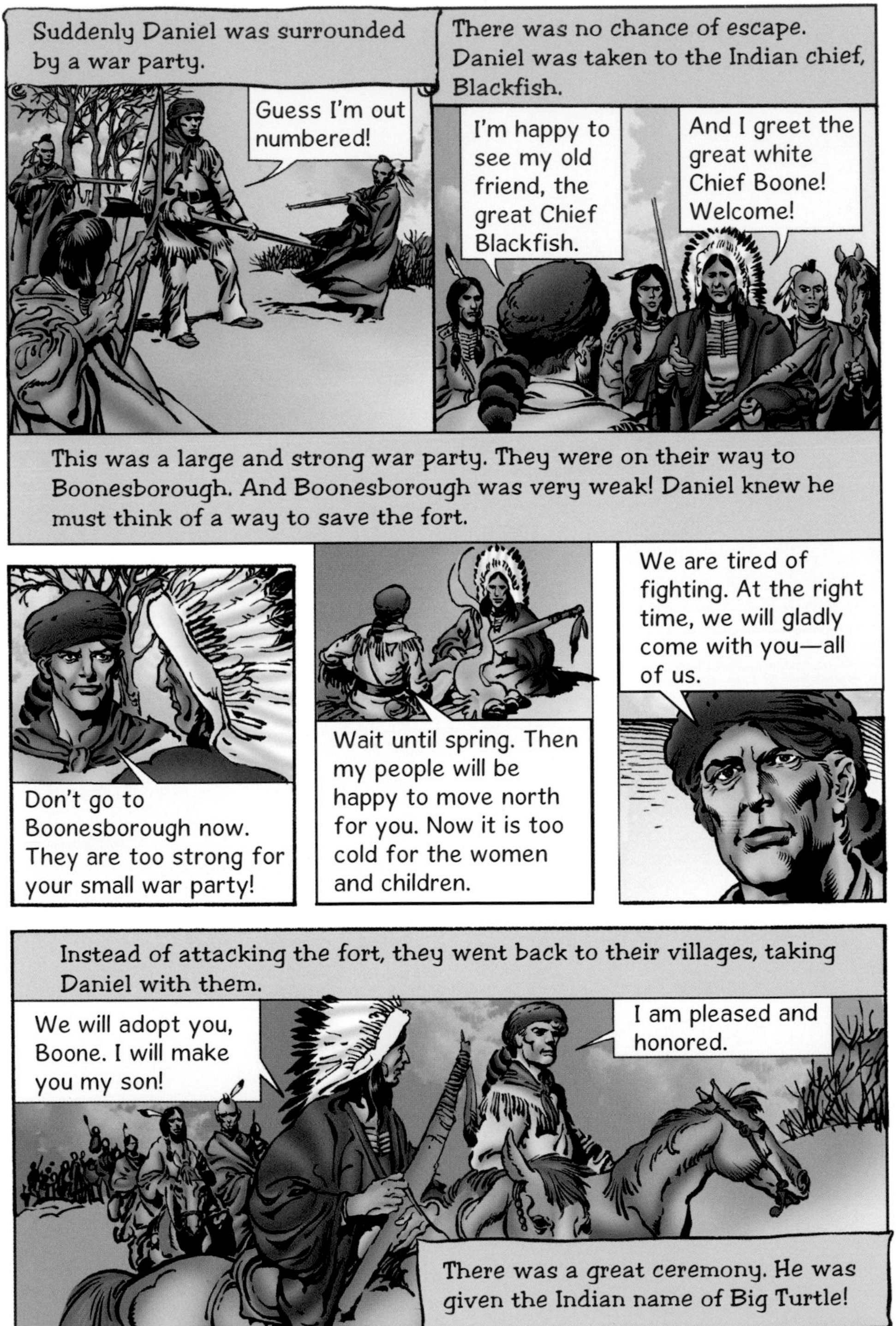
Suddenly Daniel was surrounded by a war party.
Guess I'm out numbered!
There was no chance of escape. Daniel was taken to the Indian chief, Blackfish.
I'm happy to see my old friend, the great Chief Blackfish.
And I greet the great white Chief Boone! Welcome!
This was a large and strong war party. They were on their way to Boonesborough. And Boonesborough was very weak! Daniel knew he must think of a way to save the fort.
Don't go to Boonesborough now. They are too strong for your small war party!
Wait until spring. Then my people will be happy to move north for you. Now it is too cold for the women and children.
We are tired of fighting. At the right time, we will gladly come with you—all of us.
Instead of attacking the fort, they went back to their villages, taking Daniel with them.
We will adopt you, Boone. I will make you my son!
I am pleased and honored.
There was a great ceremony. He was given the Indian name of Big Turtle!

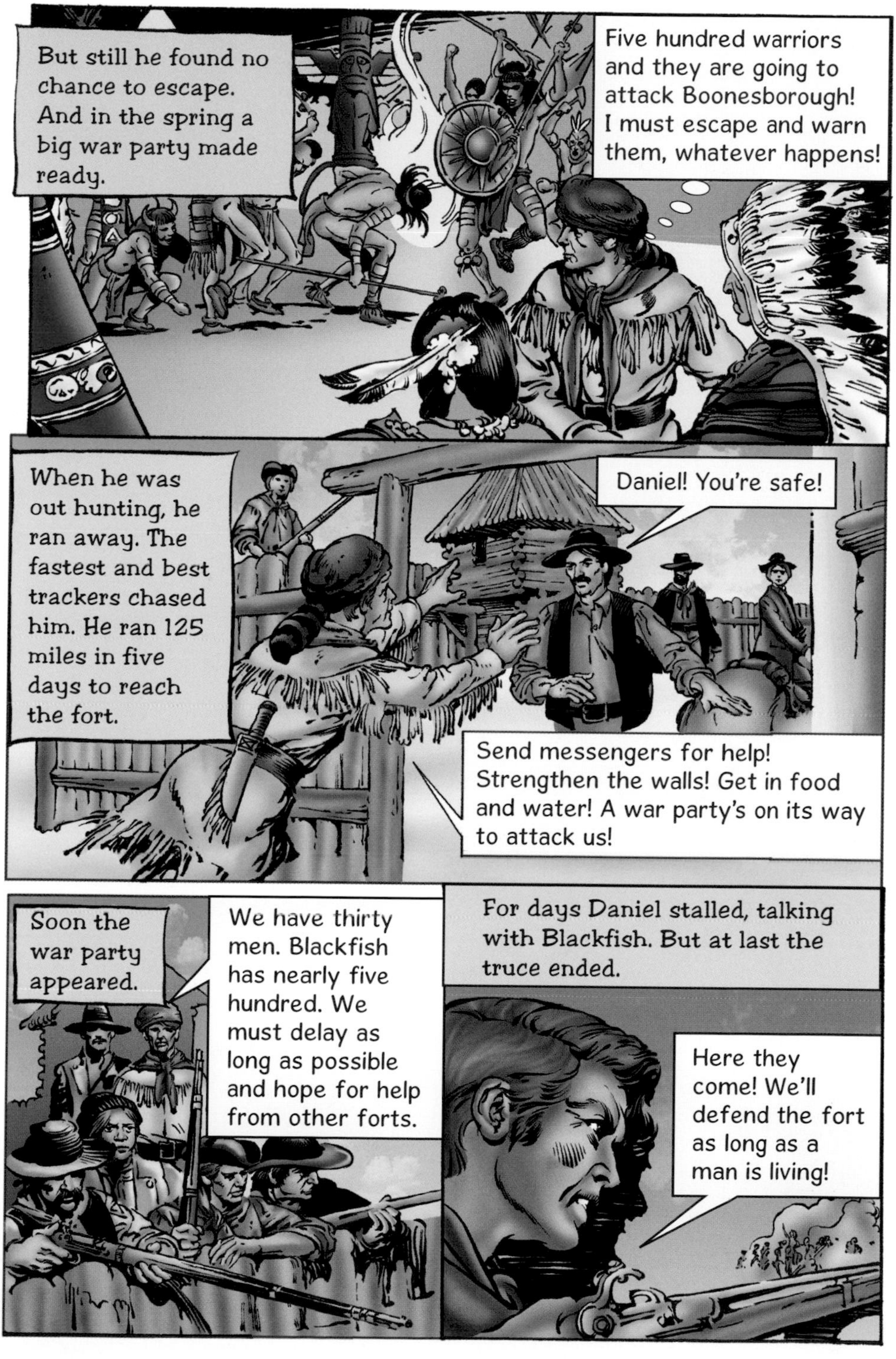
But still he found no chance to escape. And in the spring a big war party made ready.
Five hundred warriors and they are going to attack Boonesborough! I must escape and warn them, whatever happens!
When he was out hunting, he ran away. The fastest and best trackers chased him. He ran 125 miles in five days to reach the fort.
Daniel! You're safe!
Send messengers for help! Strengthen the walls! Get in food and water! A war party's on its way to attack us!
Soon the war party appeared.
We have thirty men. Blackfish has nearly five hundred. We must delay as long as possible and hope for help from other forts.
For days Daniel stalled, talking with Blackfish. But at last the truce ended.
Here they come! We'll defend the fort as long as a man is living!

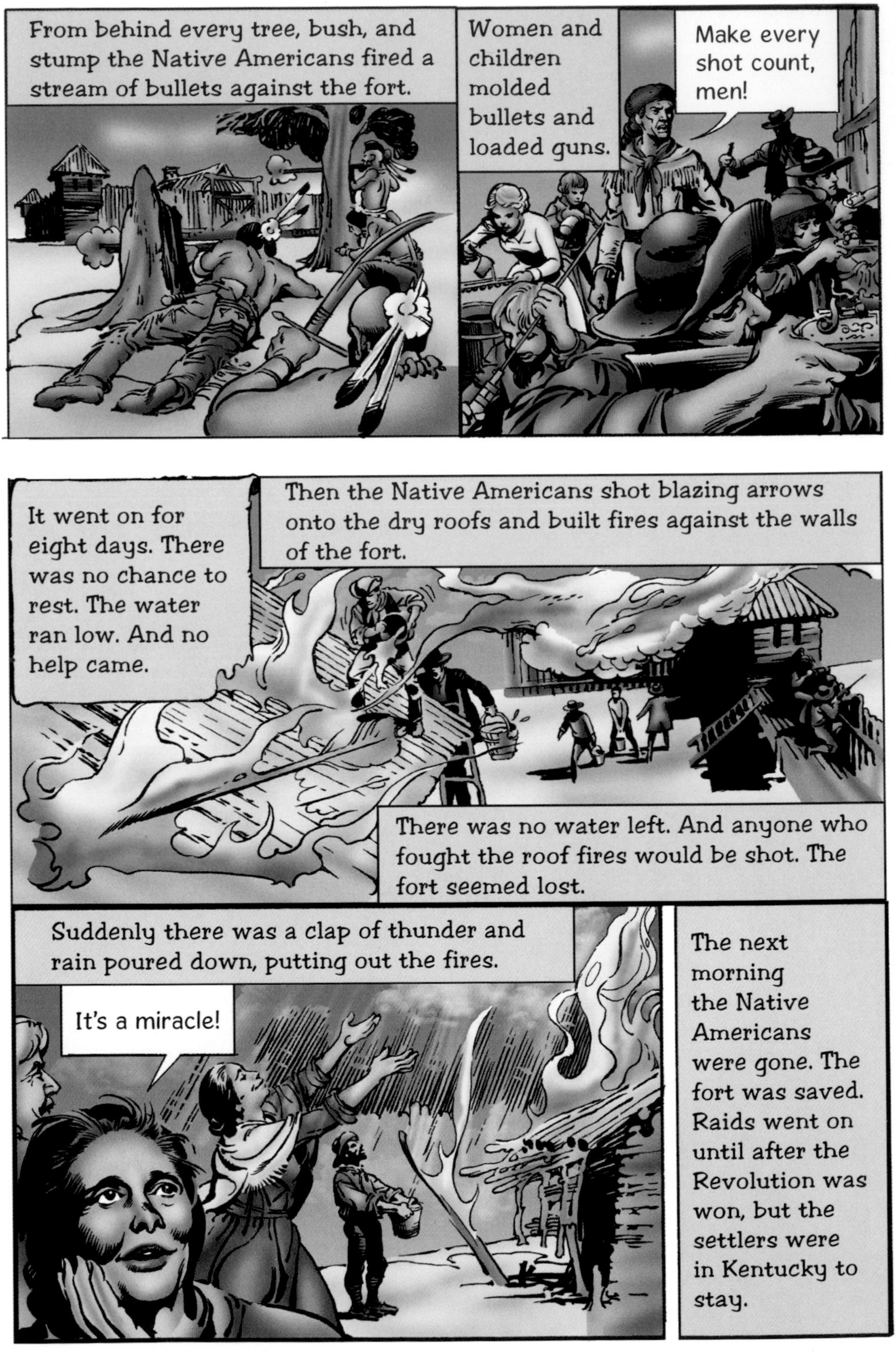
From behind every tree, bush, and stump the Native Americans fired a stream of bullets against the fort.
Women and children molded bullets and loaded guns.
Make every shot count, men!
It went on for eight days. There was no chance to rest. The water ran low. And no help came.
Then the Native Americans shot blazing arrows onto the dry roofs and built fires against the walls of the fort.
There was no water left. And anyone who fought the roof fires would be shot. The fort seemed lost.
Suddenly there was a clap of thunder and rain poured down, putting out the fires.
It's a miracle!
The next morning the Native Americans were gone. The fort was saved. Raids went on until after the Revolution was won, but the settlers were in Kentucky to stay.

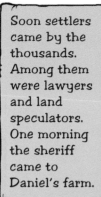

Soon settlers came by the thousands. Among them were lawyers and land speculators. One morning the sheriff came to Daniel's farm.

I'm sorry Daniel, but you don't have a legal right to own your land.

I've opened up millions of acres to settlement, fought off the Native Americans, and now they question the ownership of my few acres?

But the court said Daniel did not own the land. It was not until many years later that the U.S. Congress voted to give him 1,000 acres.

There's too many people and towns and lawyers here. Time we moved along, maybe to Missouri Territory. They say it's like Kentucky used to be.

Missouri was in the west and at that time belonged to Spain. They knew all about Daniel Boone there.

Señor Boone, we are honored to have you here! We will give you 1,000 acres of land!

They also made him a judge for the district.

Daniel lived until he was eighty-five. He was a famous man. People came from everywhere to visit him. But he never gave up exploring.

Tell us about one of your adventures, Mr. Boone.

I'd rather tell you about the West. You've seen nothing until you've seen the Rocky Mountains and Yellowstone!

THE END

Saddleback's Graphic Fiction & Nonfiction

If you enjoyed this Graphic Biography ... you will also enjoy our other graphic titles including:

Graphic Classics

- Around the World in Eighty Days
- The Best of Poe
- Black Beauty
- The Call of the Wild
- A Christmas Carol
- A Connecticut Yankee in King Arthur's Court
- Dr. Jekyll and Mr. Hyde
- Dracula
- Frankenstein
- The Great Adventures of Sherlock Holmes
- Gulliver's Travels
- Huckleberry Finn
- The Hunchback of Notre Dame
- The Invisible Man
- Jane Eyre
- Journey to the Center of the Earth
- Kidnapped
- The Last of the Mohicans
- The Man in the Iron Mask
- Moby Dick
- The Mutiny On Board H.M.S. Bounty
- The Mysterious Island
- The Prince and the Pauper
- The Red Badge of Courage
- The Scarlet Letter
- The Swiss Family Robinson
- A Tale of Two Cities
- The Three Musketeers
- The Time Machine
- Tom Sawyer
- Treasure Island
- 20,000 Leagues Under the Sea
- The War of the Worlds

Graphic Shakespeare

- As You Like It
- Hamlet
- Julius Caesar
- King Lear
- Macbeth
- The Merchant of Venice
- A Midsummer Night's Dream
- Othello
- Romeo and Juliet
- The Taming of the Shrew
- The Tempest
- Twelfth Night

SADDLEBACK
EDUCATIONAL PUBLISHING